nine inch nails

A MUSIC SERVICES PAPERBACK

This is a Carlton Book
Exclusively distributed in the U.S.A. by MSI Corporation, P.O. Box 661026,
Miami Springs, Florida 33266 - 1026.

Text and design © 1995 Carlton Books Limited
CD Guide format © 1995 Carlton Books Limited

All rights reserved. No parts of this publication may be reproduced, stored in a retrieval system, or transmitted, in any form or by any means, electronic, mechanical, photocopying, recording or otherwise, without the prior permission of the copyright owner.

ISBN 1 886894 25 6

Printed in Italy

THE AUTHOR
Jeremy Dean is an independent underground film-maker and journalist who has worked for several national magazines and newspapers.

Picture Acknowedgements
The publishers would like to thank the following sources for their kind permission to reproduce the photographs in this book:
London Features International; Pictorial Press; Range Pictures; Redferns; Retna Pictures; Rex Features; SIN.

contents

introduction 6
chapter 1: down in it 10
chapter 2: pretty hate machine 36
chapter 3: piggy in the middle 62
chapter 4: woodstock 92
chronology 114
discography 115
index 119

introduction

Nine Inch Nails are surprising, deceptive and dangerous. The image evoked by the name comes pretty close to summing up the sound: hard, metallic and with a point. They have caused quite a stir in the mainstream and college charts, with heavy metal audiences, MTV, the FBI and the British police!

Musically, main man Trent Reznor has used his Nine Inch Nails to merge industrial dancecore, traditional pop and metal in such a vital manner that the barrier between the usual cult status afforded such bands and the mainstream has been punctured. The ground-breaking debut album, *Pretty Hate Machine,* achieved major crossover success, but rather than planting easy-grow pop seeds and waiting for commercial chart success to blossom, the follow-up EP, *Broken*, was a much harder, uglier and more intense crop of songs, exploring the darker corners of sound and self. Surprisingly, the success continues!

The Nine Inch Nails (NIN) live phenomenon is intimate, aggressive and often truly dangerous. More than once, the shows have ended with

Nine Inch Nails

injury to the band, the audience, and most certainly the hardware. To watch NIN on stage is to become involved. The all-in performance demands a reaction from everyone who witnesses it. It is impossible to

Trent Reznor

remain indifferent. Ecstatic, affronted, excited, incited, disgusted—maybe all of these, but never indifferent.

Nine Inch Nails are not a traditional band: they are an ever-changing lineup centered around Trent Reznor, who is very much in control. The sound appropriates myriad elements from the fringes of modern, experimental music and mainstream rock fare. Through cutting-edge technology, Reznor hones the result into a focused and effective vehicle for lyrics that are born of severe self-contemplation and -definition.

In a world where pop has become a producer's medium and chart formulas dictate the beats per minute, duration and even the theme of singles, Nine Inch Nails are refreshingly anarchic and definitely non-conformist. Inexplicably successful in a genre where, in order to become popular, most bands willingly enslave themselves to the lowest common denominator to broaden their appeal, NIN have retained their honesty and integrity. Their sound is raw and evocative of the most subtle and extreme human feelings.

A whisper and a scream. A roar and a sigh.

> **Trent has used his Nine Inch Nails to merge industrial dancecore, pop and metal.**

down in it

Sparks fly. Metal smashes into metal. Dull leather stretches and cracks. Dyed hair leaps about part-shaved scalps. Dreadlocks and rat-tails swing. Guitars take severe punishment, howling in agony. Keyboards topple and break under the pounding of heavy booted kicks. Assorted half-eaten pizzas and opened boxes of corn starch fly into the bewildered audience. Incandescent sprays of beer and saliva glitter in the stage lights and rain on to the front rows. Anger and frustration build to breaking point and beyond. There is blood. The feedback rises to meet the pain threshold and explodes as the last string twangs and snaps. The onslaught of Nine Inch Nails implodes as Trent Reznor fights his way off stage, punching his road

> "One national news program has branded Trent 'insidious.' One of his early videos sparked an FBI murder inquiry."

Reznor—not the happiest guy in the world

manager in the mouth in his frenzy to escape. Members of the audience do not understand what they have just witnessed. This is not what they came to see. They have been scorned and abused. Yet they are impressed.

Trent Reznor, primary Nine Incher, has a reputation. One national news program has branded him "insidious." MTV shied away from screening a notorious promotional video that sparked an FBI murder inquiry into his death. He has been called a misogynist. Rumors were spread that he knew Jeffrey Dahmer. He has been linked with the late Kurt Cobain's wife, Courtney Love.

Trent has been repeatedly misrepresented, misinterpreted and misunderstood. He only ever had a platonic relationship with Courtney Love. He had no link at all to Dahmer. It angers him to be called a misogynist. He has never been murdered. Some things need to be cleared up once and for all...

birth

Michael Trent Reznor was born May 17, 1965, to parents who had both grown up in Mercer, Pennsylvania. They had been forced by circumstance into an early marriage when they were both in their teens. Young Michael was always referred to by his middle name, Trent, to differentiate him from his father, Michael Reznor, who was a commercial artist and interior designer. Mother, Nancy, was a housewife.

The first five years of Trent's life were lived against a backdrop of the Vietnam War, the assassinations of Robert Kennedy, and Martin Luther King Jnr., the fierce race riots in Detroit, the Manson Family murders, the landing of the first men on the Moon, and the divorce of his parents.

Trent has a younger sister, Tera, who is five years his junior. Shortly after her birth, Trent and Tera's parents split up and Trent was sent to live with his maternal grandparents. Though his sister was not far away, and they still got together regularly, the young Trent never shared a family household. His experience of childhood was much as it would have been if he were an only child. Bill Clark, his grandfather, was a furniture salesman who enjoyed taking Trent on cane-pole fishing trips.

Trent liked the outdoors and joined the Scouts. He would spend hours out on his skateboard. On rainy days he would stay in, building model

> With his deeply held hatred for school, Trent quickly developed a healthy disrespect for rules and regulations.

planes or playing the piano, which was always a passion, especially when he discovered that there was more to the instrument than mimicking standard tunes.

His childhood was happy enough, though he found it difficult to understand why his mother and father split up. He was plagued by severe allergies. Cats, dust, ragweed, grass, corn, detergents—all brought his flesh out in ruddy rashes or aggravated his breathing. He also had some serious problems with his ears and hearing. He had to have a series of operations to drain fluid and relieve pressure against his eardrums.

> Trent's favorite TV program was *The Six Million Dollar Man*. To this day, Trent often goes under the name Steve Austin when he's traveling.

school

Family structure and the early schooling process have an important part to play in the imprinting of respect for authority. Trent hated going to school. Without what many would consider a normal, nuclear family background and with his deeply held hatred for school, Trent quickly developed a healthy disrespect for rules and regulations. His

CHAPTER ONE: DOWN IN IT

grandparents were caring, though not strict, and the young Reznor found himself with more freedom than was afforded most children of his age.

He was a loner as a teenager, fascinated with science fiction. His favorite TV show was *The Six Million Dollar Man.* To this day, Trent often goes under the name of Steve Austin when traveling incognito. This innocent escapism took a more sinister turn when he discovered horror in the extreme form of the movies *The Exorcist* and *The Omen*. Trent felt the

Off the rails after being on the right tracks

Trent's first stage performance was as Judas in Jesus Christ Superstar!

power of the archetypal demon child, Damien. He wanted to believe in something else. He wanted to make a deal with the devil. He was powerless to prevent his parents splitting up. Trent was the object of schoolyard ridicule because of his quiet nature, his allergies and because he had to wear a bathing cap when swimming due to his infected ears. There had to be something more.

> Trent's father introduced his 14-year-old son to illegal drugs when they shared a marijuana joint.

Trent was raised Protestant and was regularly sent to Sunday School. Trent had started learning the piano when he was five, around the time his parents split, and later took lessons for the saxophone and tuba. He joined junior high marching bands and a school jazz band. His interest in rock music took off when his fascination with horror and science fiction met its match in the music of Kiss. The group's lead singer, Gene Simmons, was his boyhood hero. Trent found the whole rock image seductive and fascinating.

Trent's first stage appearances were in school drama productions, when he played Judas in *Jesus Christ Superstar*, and the title role in *The Music Man*. He was voted "Best In Drama" by a poll of his fellow students at Mercer Area High School.

After the turmoil of his parents' split had settled a little, Trent and his father became like best friends. His father introduced his 14-year-old son to illegal drugs when they shared a marijuana joint. Trent maintains that his father was pretty much responsible for the way he turned out. He was always supportive of his son's creative tendencies, buying him guitars and providing encouragement and inspiration. Trent helped out at an acoustic musical instrument store that his father ran and was soon jamming with other local kids. He became involved with a few local Mercer bands, including Option 30. He went on to join a covers band, The Urge, which played a couple of clubs, then joined Slam Bam Boo and Lucky Pierre (which also featured Kevin McMahon of Prick).

> When the movie, *Light Of Day*, was filmed in Cleveland, Trent was offered a part as a member of the band, The Problems.

To this day, there is often a middle-aged man in the audience at NIN gigs. A man who at first glance appears to be a roadie, or maybe a manager. Slim, with his hair tied back into a pony tail, watching the riotous audience with barely concealed glee. This is Michael Reznor Snr., Trent Reznor's dad...

work

After graduating from high school in 1983, Trent studied computer engineering and music at Allegheny college. It only took a year to confirm his desire to play music and he dropped out of college. He struck out on his own and moved to Cleveland, Ohio, in 1984 where he successfully auditioned to join a band called The Innocents as their keyboard player. They were a typical teenage combo, flashy, juvenile and a product of that moment's fashion. He was with them for just three months, during which time they secured a short-lived record deal. He did not play on any of the tracks selected for their album, *Livin' On The Street*, though his picture did feature on the packaging.

Trent combined his skill and interest in music by getting a job at the Right Track recording studios—now known as Midtown Recording. Working as engineer and general gopher, he waxed floors and did odd jobs as well as helping with the technical side of recording the local bands who used the studios. He quickly won the trust and support of the studio boss, Bart Koster, and was given permission to stay after work to use the recording facilities.

When the movie, *Light Of Day*, starring Michael J. Fox and Joan Jett, was filmed in Cleveland, Trent was offered a small part playing a member of a band named The Problems—a typical Eighties new wave set up who performed a reworked version of the Buddy Holly song 'True Love Ways' in the movie. At this time, Trent was also playing with a band called The Exotic Birds, who got as far as sending out demo tapes.

> After running through pages of potential names in his notebook, Trent eventually settled on Nine Inch Nails.

By now, he had already begun writing his own songs. He was heavily into The Clash, so naturally he attempted to emulate their style with politically charged lyrics. Eventually, he discovered that it was when he was being honest about his own personal feelings, that his songs were more successful. He became introverted and began scrutinizing his innermost desires, urges and fears. The lyrics began to feel more real, carry more weight, mean more to himself and others. He began to take sections from his personal journals and adapt the words into songs. He identified elements he believed to hold truths and reexpressed them in ways that were personally moving to him. He found that they were to others, too.

Trent worked alone during the night, taking advantage of Bart Koster's offer to use the Right Track studio. When he was not working or using the studio's facilities, he would hole up in his basement and work there. He taught himself to use the computer sampling and composing software to create the sounds he heard in his head.

> **Some say the name Nine Inch Nails is a sexual innuendo relating to a certain part of Trent's anatomy.**

After running through pages of potential names in his notebook, Trent eventually settled on Nine Inch Nails. It was a tough, aggressive name. Two weeks later, it still sounded good to him, so it stuck. There are a few theories as to the name's origin and true meaning. One is that the Statue of Liberty's hands are carved with fingernails that are nine inches long. Another is that the nails used to crucify Jesus were nine inches in length.

Clint Ruin putting some nine-inch nails to use

CHAPTER ONE: DOWN IN IT

The artist formerly a big influence on NIN

Nine-inch nails are sometimes used to fix down the lids of burial caskets. Some say the name is a sexual innuendo relating to the length of a certain part of Trent's anatomy... Trent remains enigmatic.

He worked in this very focused and self-centered way, creating a collection of tracks that would make up the first NIN album. This solitary writing process allowed Trent to tap into his deepest core and draw upon his emotions, desires, fears and insecurities. He found that the

Trent listened to U.K. songsters XTC

things that irritated him the most also motivated him—anger and frustration became his most potent tools. Trent's musical influences were, by now, many and varied: he listened to Ministry for their intensity and aggression; he still had a soft spot for the songwriting of XTC; he held the production values of Severed Heads in very high esteem, and he enjoyed listening to the near-perfectly crafted pop of Prince.

During the latter stages of recording a demo tape, he enlisted the help of his

A severed head with production values

Reznor—down in it

roommate Chris Vrenna (who had been working consistently with Chicago dancecore gurus Die Warsau), and soon they were sending out the first batch of NIN songs. They were about to sign a management deal with John Malm.

'Down In It' was the first song that Trent had enough confidence in to record and release. NIN's debut single appeared on 12-inch vinyl in 1987. Appropriately, the lyrics explore what appears to be a suicide fantasy. Not a suicide note, a fantasy—something which almost everyone goes through at least once in a while. This potentially negative set of thoughts and emotions had been turned around by the creative process into a kind of redemption hymn by the very fact that it had spurred the creativity within. Trent has explained the meaning of the song in various ways in interviews and live introductions—it either concerns death or sex. Somehow, this felt more real than when he addressed a political theme with intellect. These

> 'Down In It' concerns death or sex… personal thoughts that were unnervingly close to the heart.

NIN live—in the early days

personal thoughts were unnervingly close to the heart—honest and raw emotion. It was effective.

Approximately ten demos went out and NIN were offered eight record contracts. Though Reznor did not immediately leap into any of the offered deals, they boosted his confidence enough to take on a tour supporting hardcore electro band, Skinny Puppy. Reznor admired Skinny Puppy very much, so this was a real acid test: to be thrown in at the deep end.

> NIN went on tour supporting unlikely acts, including ex-Bauhaus star Peter Murphy and U.K. indie guitar band, The Wonderstuff.

For the tour, Trent had to select a group of musicians who could produce music true to his internal model of what NIN should be. He had removed himself from the Cleveland scene for a while and taken a trip to London, England. There he put an advertisement in U.K. music journals such as *Melody Maker*. None of the hundred or more musicians who responded were on his wavelength, so he returned to Cleveland and put together a few young

Trent was used to solitary work

CHAPTER ONE: DOWN IN IT

and impressionable players who were eager and open to his ideas and suggestions.

NIN went on to fill the support slot for a series of more unlikely acts, including ex-Bauhaus and Goth Shocker Peter Murphy. They even found themselves opening for U.K. indie guitar band, The Wonder Stuff. This short-lived tour opportunity ended with a stage full of shattered instruments and a bloody-mouthed road manager attempting to bring a freaked-out Trent back to normality.

> "When I wrote *Pretty Hate Machine*, I thought 'What would be my reason for having a band?'"
> **TRENT ON NIN'S FIRST ALBUM**

By now, Reznor and Vrenna were living in a decrepit old house in the ghetto area of Cleveland. They were already experimenting with image and appearance, resulting in much harassment from many intolerant locals. This kind of reaction only served to strengthen their resolve to do what they had set out to do: create a band with a confrontational and aggressive approach.

Reznor signed to Steve Gottlieb's TVT records, one of the eight labels that had shown an interest in the demo he submitted. Trent was now

NIN—eager and open to suggestion

CHAPTER ONE: DOWN IN IT

confronted with the task of turning the months of intense creativity, self examination, song writing, playing and mixing into a set of songs good enough for a debut album.

Trent exclusively wrote, arranged and programmed *Pretty Hate Machine*. Originally, he had wanted to retain total control over the production side of the album, enlisting only the technical talent of the highly respected producer, Flood, who had worked with Depeche Mode (one of the USA's most successful tour bands), Nitzer Ebb, Erasure, and Crime & The City Solution, among many others. Instead, he found himself confronted with an impressive lineup of some of the most renowned producers working in the contemporary scene: Adrian Sherwood of the On-U Sound set up who had worked with the likes of Ministry, Cabaret Voltaire, Kein Mitleid Fuer Die Mehrheit (KMFDM or No Mercy For The Masses), and Depeche Mode; John Fryer the man behind Love & Rockets, He Said, Wire, Cocteau Twins; Keith LeBlanc who had worked with Tackhead, Fats Comet, Barmy Army, Maffia; and Flood!

Reznor said of the album, "When I wrote *Pretty Hate Machine*, I thought, 'What would be my reason for having a band? What can I say musically or lyrically?' I was looking inward and made some very personal songs that were about how I felt about certain things. The motivation was more dissatisfaction rather than, 'I'm the happiest guy in the world—let's write an album!'

"The theme of the record revealed itself to be things that were really bothering me: not

> "Our live show has gotten a lot more aggressive than the records. My whole idea of a performance is to take it beyond just being a band on stage."
> **TRENT**

having my religious outlook together, not being able to fit neatly into a little hole in society, trouble dealing with people on a one-to-one basis. Nothing staggeringly new, teenage angst, but trying to do it with some sincerity, a kind of questioning self examination."

death

From the finished set of ten songs which made up Nine Inch Nails' 1989 debut album, *Pretty Hate Machine*, TVT decided that 'Down In It' should be the track selected to showcase the album. 'Down In It' certainly gave the U.S. charts a hammering, charging to Number 1 on *Rolling Stone*'s Dance Chart and ripping into the Top 20 on *Billboard*'s Club Charts. It was noticed and a happy accident, involving corn starch, a super eight camera, balloons and a Midwest farmer, was to bring the name of Trent Reznor to an even wider audience—including the FBI, who launched a murder inquiry to find Trent's killers!?

So, by the time Trent Reznor was 30 years of age, he had lived the rock star lifestyle to its fullest extent. The sex, the drugs, he even died young... and is still around to tell the tale. And will tell the tale many times yet.

pretty hate machine

Rumors of Reznor's death were greatly exaggerated. What started as a mishap during the filming of an early video for the first NIN single blew out of all proportion and was to prove more effective than the cleverest publicity stunt. This could not have been planned! No way.

Trent and friends were experimenting with lowering Super-Eight cameras off buildings. The theme of the video, very obliquely, was suicide. The track was 'Down In It', which is not primarily about suicide at all, but when juxtaposed with that idea in a self-crucifixion parody, makes sense. They were attempting to film a scene where Trent was lying on the ground with corn starch on his face to give a semblance of death. The camera was attached to a weather balloon filled with helium.

A string was also attached to the balloon, so when it was released, carrying the rolling camera skyward, it would be retrievable. When the film was reversed, it would look like the camera was dropping downward toward Trent's head.

What actually happened was that the string slipped its knot and the contraption took off! All they could do was watch as it drifted higher and higher, disappearing over the horizon. Trent recalls hoping that it would not drop out of the sky and hit someone on the head! Then thought nothing more of it.

> The FBI requested that Trent fly back to Chicago to prove that he was who he said, and to convince them that he was still living.

A year later, Trent's manager, John Malm, heard from the FBI. The camera had drifted 200 miles across the stratosphere before landing in the middle of a Michigan corn field. The farmer who found it thought he had come across some kind of drug surveillance camera and took it to the local police. The police developed the film and they saw the images of a young man lying apparently dead, surrounded by what seemed to be

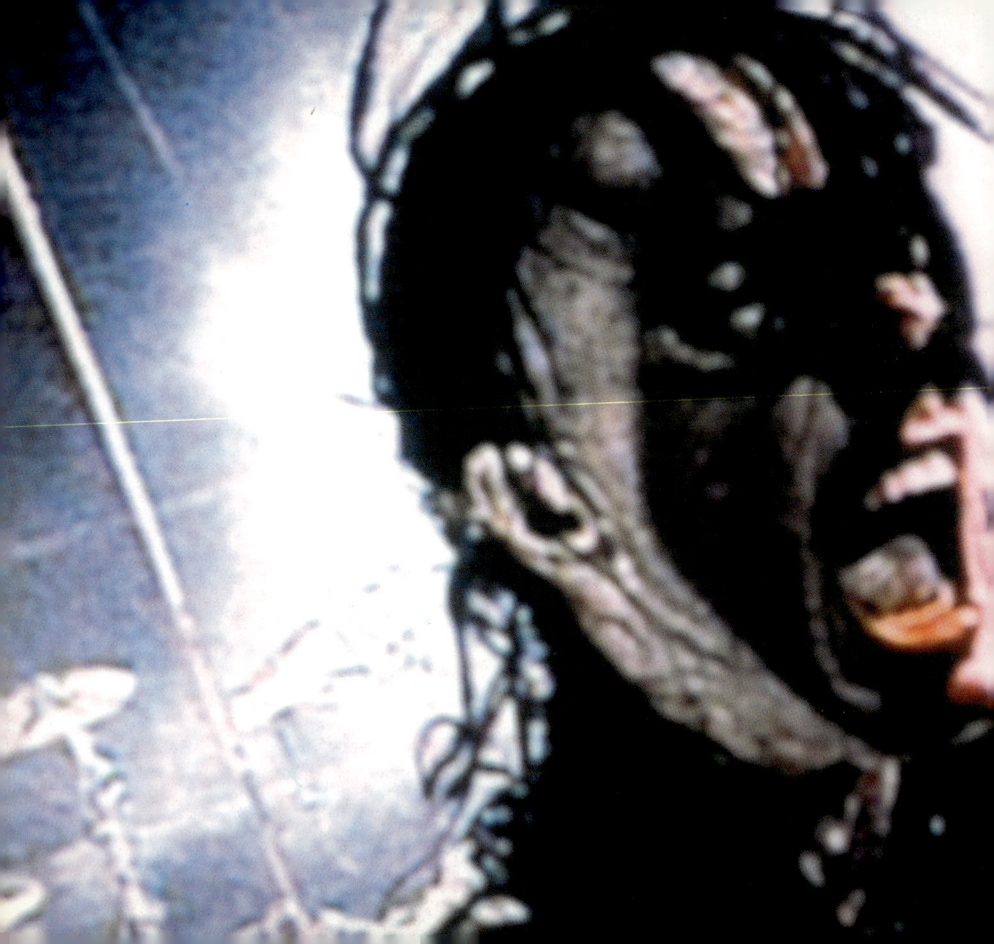

CHAPTER TWO: PRETTY HATE MACHINE

a strange looking gang. The police somehow reached the conclusion that they had uncovered some kind of snuff film with a clue to a killing and brought in the FBI for a full-blown murder inquiry.

Through visual clues they were able to track its origins to Chicago, where it was filmed. There they put out an appeal for any information concerning the victim's identity. A local art student recognized the lead singer of Nine Inch Nails and informed the police. The FBI requested that Trent fly back to Chicago to prove that he was who he claimed to be and to convince them that he was still living. Then, they realized how farcical the whole

Head like a hole!

scenario was and put the 12-month police operation down to experience. Trent Reznor is the kind of guy things happen to.

lollapalooza

The whole story broke around the time of the first Lollapalooza tour in 1991, just in time to tie in with the PR campaign for the 1990 follow-up single, 'Head Like A Hole' from *Pretty Hate Machine*. Trent had constructed a formidable live lineup for NIN consisting of James Woolley, formerly of Die Warsau, the late Jeff Ward of Jello Biafra's band Lard, and Richard Patrick. The live format had become even more focused and intense. Trent now avoided drinking alcohol before shows, allowing him to project his tortured emotions and imaginings unfiltered into the heart of the audience. The sense of danger and confrontation was heightened as Trent stripped away the distance between performer and onlooker, breaking down the usual barriers of ego and awe. The audience became part of the show, the atmosphere electrified. Adrenalin pumped on and offstage simultaneously. Reznor's lyric, "This is the only time I really feel alive," could well apply here.

> "Ice-T was a totally cool guy, very talented."
> **TRENT ON LOLLAPALOOZA**

"This is the only time I feel alive."

NIN start to get aggressive

CHAPTER TWO: PRETTY HATE MACHINE

Trent commented, "Our live show has gotten a lot more aggressive than the records. My whole idea of a performance is to take it beyond just being a band on stage. I've noticed in our shows that when they get more chaotic, people like it. And the greater the element of danger to the audience—not that we're gonna attack them and kill them—then there's real interest being inspired and their attention is focused. The music excites them and the energy released is interactive."

Nine Inch Nails were able to reach a wider audience on the Lollapalooza tour, often billed between varied breakthrough acts like Jane's Addiction and Ice-T, who once joined them on stage to play guitar on 'Head Like A Hole'! As Trent recalls, "Ice-T was a totally cool guy, very talented. We were still an up-and-coming thing. The biggest show we'd ever played was 200 people. Now we're in front of this scary, potentially hostile audience of 25,000. I was afraid the other bands might be into this star thing, *'I want catering!'* But everybody—

> "I was afraid the other bands might be into this star thing. But everybody except Henry Rollins was very friendly."
> **TRENT**

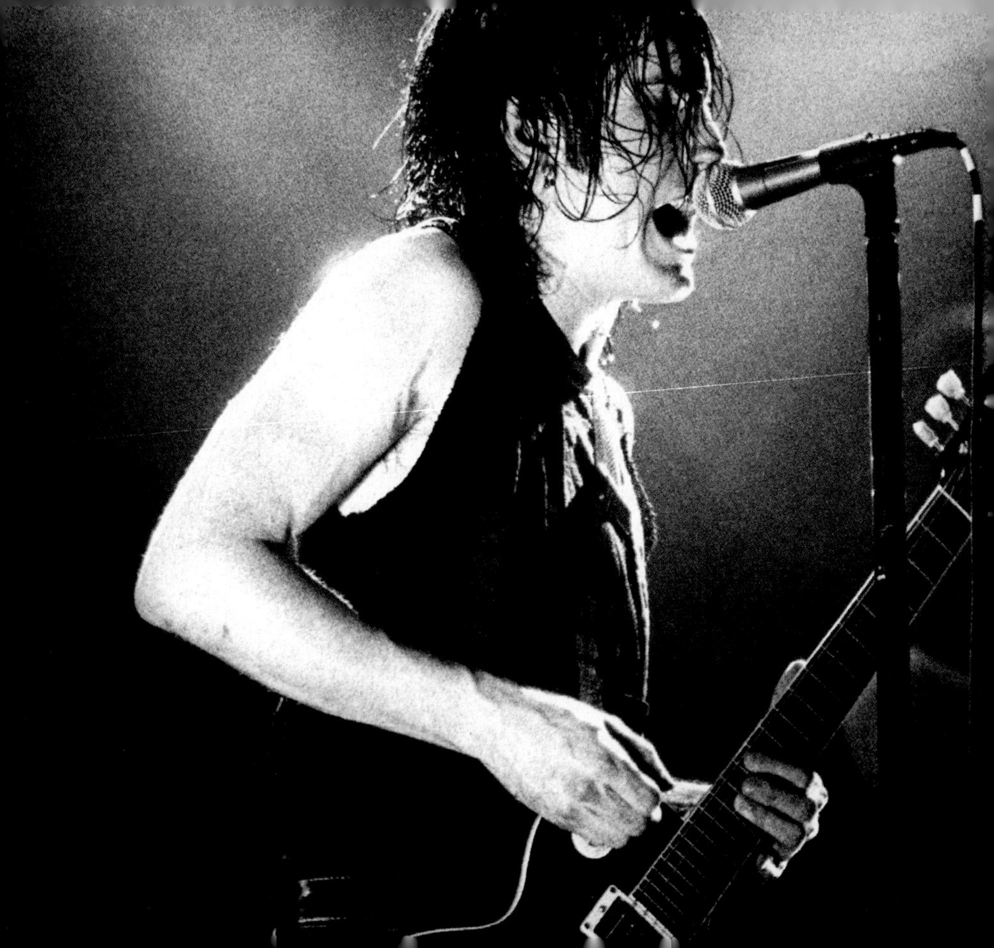

CHAPTER TWO: PRETTY HATE MACHINE

with the exception of Henry Rollins—was very friendly."

The tour also brought them to the favorable attention of Axl Rose, resulting in an invitation to open for Guns N' Roses on a short tour of major European venues. The high point for NIN was their live debut in the U.K. at London's famous Wembley Stadium, opening for one of the world's biggest rock outfits in front of a sell-out 85,000 crowd!

The oddity of what was basically a synth act supporting a guitar-oriented rock band only added to the impact. NIN laid huge slabs of noise over what were primarily pop rock structures and, surprisingly, were well received. Trent said of the experience: "It was what I'd expected, and worse. Axl's a friend of mine, we met in LA when he asked if

The onslaught begins

we wanted to open for Guns N' Roses on some dates in America. We couldn't do it, but as we were planning on going over to Europe, we thought what better and stranger way to do it than supporting the biggest rock band in the world? I don't care if people want to think we're cock rock..."

Nine Inch Nails used the spectacular event as a springboard for their own headlining tour of Europe. At their U.K. gig at the London Astoria, they certainly attracted the attention of the

Axl Rose—cock rock?

CHAPTER TWO: PRETTY HATE MACHINE

British press. The next day a journalist filed a complaint with the police and was taking legal advice on suing Reznor for assault. The journalist alleged that he had been hit on the head by a bottle flung from the stage during the explosive set, resulting in a black eye. It seemed unlikely that the flying bottle had originated from the stage as NIN tend only to throw things at each other—like synths, amplifiers and guitars! Besides, Trent would have to have one hell of a pitching arm to launch an object up to the balcony, where the collision of cranium and bottle apparently occurred.

> "Axl's a friend of mine, we met in LA when he asked if we wanted to open for Guns N' Roses on some dates."
> **TRENT**

As it turned out, the charges were dropped and Trent was able to fly back to New Orleans—delayed only when the plane he was on had to make a forced landing after part of the cockpit window ruptured during the flight. Trent Reznor is the kind of guy things happen to.

By this time, Nine Inch Nails had already established their own very solid fan base. *Pretty Hate Machine* was selling faster than the shelves of

Cyberpunk!

CHAPTER TWO: PRETTY HATE MACHINE

many a record store could be restocked. After trimming the 'Down In It' video because it could be interpreted as containing a suicide theme, MTV were wary of screening the video for the second single, 'Head Like A Hole' because of its violent imagery. Reluctantly, they allowed it to be screened a couple of times. It soon became an MTV standard.

cyberpunk

The key to NIN's surprise success is the wide

> **Reznor hit the headlines when a British journalist attempted to sue him for assault after NIN's gig at the London Astoria.**

crossover appeal of the sound. There is enough intensity and integrity to satisfy the hardcore followers. The songs retain elements of pop structure and memorable chorus structures for the more general rock fan. The harshness of the sampled sounds and jack hammer rhythms appeal to followers of industrial dancecore. The innovative abuse of instruments and inventive electronic sound manipulation is enough to keep the aficionados of arty experimental music occupied. The themes of alienation and destructive desires may be pretty standard rock'n'roll fare, but the blunt and blatant honesty of Trent's lyrics bring renewed fascination.

Nine Inch Nails were already the premier cyber-

Timothy Leary—the happiest guy in the world

punks of the music scene. Cyberpunk was a new term then, a phrase coined in the late-Eighties. Dr Timothy Leary, high priest of cyberculture whose fame originated in the Sixties, when he achieved notoriety as *the* Harvard Acid Guru, referred to by William Gibson, science fiction hotshot author of *Neuromancer,* as a cyberpunk. New York band Sonic Youth used the phrase to describe their brand of bubble gum noise assault. Cyberpunk was most readily associated with the smash action movie of the Eighties, *RoboCop*, which packed a punch right through to the cinema mainstream.

> The grunge phenomenon of the early-Nineties was to the USA what punk had been to Europe a decade earlier.

The earliest manifestation of the cyberpunk ethos must have been *The Cybernauts*, an episode of the cult Sixties British TV series, *The Avengers*, followed by the bionic Steve Austin in *The Six Million Dollar Man.* Central to the cyberpunk ethos is the theme of the individual, almost entirely swamped by automation and artificial social structures, winning through against the evil of the powers that be. These are pertinent fables in this age of information technology

Nirvana— grunge's finest

and a world controlled by multi-national corporations and banks. Although the elements of the genre are hard-hitting graphic violence and a total disregard for genteel sensibilities, there always has to be an underlying comment on humanity or society.

American youth had been primed by the explosion of the Seattle grunge scene to accept harder, noisier rock music laced with the lyrics of dissatisfaction. Bands like Soundgarden, Pearl Jam and Nirvana ripped up the charts with hefty guitar riffs and an anti-establishment tone. The world's music press lapped it up. The grunge phenomenon of the early-Nineties was to the USA what punk had been to Europe a decade earlier.

> Many parallels have been drawn between Cobain and Reznor. They were both raised in small town USA and were products of broken homes

Also, the simultaneous underground resurgence of hard-line dance music had made heavy electro percussion more acceptable. NIN were a timely happening and the inability to pigeonhole their style of sonic terrorism crossed over musical borders, instead of making them more difficult to market.

Grunge was, of course, just a word: a term dreamt up by the music industry in order to market a set of bands that had found unexpected success but were difficult to stereotype. An update of the punk ploy. Though the grunge trip certainly opened doors for Nine Inch Nails, their rise to stadium stardom was overshadowed by that of the Seattle set. Because of this, they are inevitably compared. Perhaps, now more than ever.

> "Trent would have mowed lawns rather than make another record for TVT."
> **JOHN MALM ON THE RIFT BETWEEN TRENT AND TVT**

It was at this time that Reznor found himself in demand as a producer and guest musician for other potential breakthrough acts including Megadeth, Butthole Surfers, Wolfgang Press, Crunch-O-Matic, 1000 Homo DJs, Curve, KMFDM, Machines Of Loving Grace, Marilyn Manson, Ministry and Prick. He was also an active member of the amorphous "super group" Pigface, which even performed songs (such as 'Suck') that subsequently appeared as NIN tracks. Trent was heavily involved with the debut Pigface album, *Gub*, contributing the track 'Bushmaster', and helping with the engineering and recording. He also toured with them for a short period—some say he was kicked out for attempting to take control of the set up.

becoming

Reznor's prolific involvement with other acts on various record labels eventually led to resentment and contractual problems with NIN's label TVT. Trent is rumored to have worked with many more acts, but was prevented from being credited. The resentment magnified and became mutual. Just at the time when the TVT label were desperate to release a follow-up album to feed the market created by *Pretty Hate Machine*, Trent went into a professional sulk and refused to comply. Manager John Malm has said of that period, "Trent would have mowed lawns rather than make another record for TVT."

Steve Gottlieb, who originally signed NIN to TVT, blames himself for the rift that formed, admitting that, "Our relationship got dysfunctional. I obviously let Trent down. We're talking about the guy who wrote the lyric, 'I'd rather die, than give you control'!" Though Gottlieb did not let Nine Inch Nails off the hook without a contractual tussle...

Trent found no hole for his pigeon

CHAPTER TWO: PRETTY HATE MACHINE

The ensuing litigation process spanned two years and ended with Jimmy Iovine, president of Interscope records, buying out TVT in order to acquire NIN. Part of that deal included allowing Reznor to set up his own record label, to be called Nothing.

Unknown to Gottlieb, Trent had written and recorded the mini album, *Broken*, in total secrecy during the two-year legal battle. Although this was not the commercially viable sequel to *Pretty Hate Machine*, Interscope released it without qualms. Incredibly, it hit big time.

Broken was defiantly non-commercial, so it is all the more surprising that it confirmed the popularity and mainstream acceptance of Nine Inch Nails. It was six dark slabs of harsh noise, with only three of the tracks carrying any lyrics. Its release was accompanied by a video produced in collaboration with Peter Christopherson. The visuals featured

> "It's a fuck you record."
> TRENT ON *BROKEN*, THE ALBUM HE RECORDED IN VARIOUS SECRET LOCATIONS.

extreme images of pain and torture. Its ugliness reflects the period in which it was birthed. Trent recorded *Broken* in various secret locations to keep knowledge of its existence from TVT. Some editions of the record carry two bonus tracks: 'Physical (You're so)', originally performed by Adam And The Ants—a little light relief maybe—and 'Suck', which made its debut on the *Pigface* album. Trent described the project as a "fuck you record." It was even given a Grammy Award.

Trent said that *Broken* marks phase three of Nine Inch Nails, "The Becoming," which begs the question of what constitutes the first two phases? Phase one must be the origins of NIN, with *Pretty Hate Machine* documenting his conquest of any insecurities that had been preventing him from writing and performing his own songs. The revelation that he could turn his private hang ups into something worthy that others could relate to.

> "I'd seen myself mutate into something I really didn't like." TRENT ON THE POWER HE HAD OVER HIS AUDIENCE.

Phase two may have been the metamorphosis of Trent's stage persona from a wild, abusive outpouring of hate and resentment, into the unflinchingly focused and dedicated performer. He has admitted that the power he had over his audience had become corrupt and that he was, "misusing it badly. Hurting, being really shitty to people—I'd seen myself mutate into something I really didn't like."

Reznor had also been scouting talent for his Nothing record label and had signed Marilyn Manson, Prick, Coil and Pop Will Eat Itself. The label is based in the Tremont area of Cleveland, Ohio, not too far away from where he used to help with the engineering at the Right Track. Trent commented that, "at some point, I would like to focus on production, which I would really like to do more of, but Nine Inch Nails eats up every second of my life."

> "At some point, I would like to focus on production... but Nine Inch Nails eats up every second of my life."
> **TRENT**

Broken was promptly followed by *Fixed*. An allegorical nod toward his own transition from one record label to another. From a bad situation to a better one. *Fixed* was another six-track mini-album containing remixed versions of the songs from *Broken*. Trent made full use of this new opportunity to work with a set of other artists he

JG Thirwell aka Clint Ruin

CHAPTER TWO: PRETTY HATE MACHINE

particularly admired. Peter Christopherson, of Coil and formerly of the seminal Throbbing Gristle and Psychic TV—when he was known as "Sleazy Peter C"—remixed the track 'Gave Up'. JG Thirwell (AKA Clint Ruin) remixed 'Wish' and created 'Fist Fuck' from the same elements. Thirwell is probably one of the most influential figures on the production side of the industrial hardcore noise scene, from his own bands Foetus and Wiseblood, to his work with other artcore talents such as Lydia Lunch, Sonic Youth, Einsturzende Neubauten, Marc Almond, and Nick Cave. The other tracks were remixed by Reznor, Vrenna, Butch Vig and PK.

Again, the record was an inexplicable mainstream success! After two years of self-enforced cold turkey, Trent finally got his fix.

> "I'd like to break down all these stereotypes that if you're in a band, you put out a record... go on tour... and repeat the process until you have nothing else to say and die out."
> **TRENT**

piggy in the middle

Trent had been taking it easy, living in New Orleans for a short time. The city was becoming the place for radical rockers to retreat. Lydia Lunch had a hide-out there, along with Jim Thirwell. It was a place so far away from trendy West Coast haunts and New York's Soho or Greenwich Village, that it was possible to be unknown and unnoticed.

After the time of recuperation, getting used to the new-found freedom granted him by Interscope records, Trent realized the time had come to create the next full-length album. This would be no mean task: Nine Inch Nails had a lot to live up to now. He did not want to produce an easy follow up to *Pretty Hate Machine*. He had experimented with the mini-album, and achieved success on his own terms. This time he wanted to

Evidence of hardware abuse

Another use for some nine-inch nails—the Cenobites from Clive Barker's Hellraiser

make a set of songs that took ideas in different directions, yet hung together as one entity. In other words, a concept album.

To many this may have been a surprise. Trent had outlined his basic aims some time before: "I'd like to break down all these stereotypes and ideas that if you're in a band, you put out a record, hopefully once a year, and then you go on tour, and then do an album, make a video, and repeat the process until you have nothing else to say and die out."

> "A lot of people thought I'd become fascinated with serial killers." TRENT ON THE GOSSIP WHEN HE MOVED INTO THE MANSON MANSION

murder

Midway through 1992, Trent set out to find a new base in which to build his studio and work intensively in his hermit-like manner. He checked out numerous properties in the Los Angeles region until he found one that he really liked: a big, beautiful house with a spectacular view of the city of LA, and a relatively low price tag. The house was situated in the Hollywood Hills at 10050 Cielo Drive.

Dark fantasy fiction affected Trent's look

CHAPTER THREE PIGGY IN THE MIDDLE

It was the house where Sharon Tate and four guests were gruesomely butchered by members of the Manson Family on August 9, 1969. Reznor did not realize this when he signed the real estate deal and moved in. When he found out, though, it did not faze him too much. For all his fascination with the darker areas of the human psyche, Trent would in no way idolize Charles Manson, or condone his ideas, though he did find it spookily cool to be connected with an interesting chapter in American history. After all, Manson is one of the icons of the Sixties and Trent Reznor is the kind of guy things happen to.

The property had been on the market for some time. The late, great author Charles Bukowski, wrote in his autobiographical novel, *Hollywood*, an account of how he was shown around the house. He recounts how it had seemed familiar, how he had got bad feelings about it brought on by a vague inkling that he had seen the place somewhere before, in connection with some terrible event. It was only after he had left the

> "I didn't want to box NIN into a corner, where everything had to be faster and harder than the last record."
> **TRENT**

The late Sharon Tate

CHAPTER THREE: PIGGY IN THE MIDDLE

premises that it dawned on him that it was *that* house...

"A lot of people thought I'd become fascinated with serial killers," Trent explained openly, "Which I'm not. It's more about questioning my own motives. Like in *Silence Of The Lambs* or *Red Dragon*, where the scariest thing is when the detective

> It is said that the walls of one room [of the Manson house] still bore the stains where the word "pig" had been scrawled in human blood.

realizes that he has this side of his brain where he could figure out what the killer could be doing. Because he has part of that in him."

It is said that the walls of one room still bore the stains where the word "pig" had been scrawled in human blood. This is the room Trent chose to convert into the nucleus of his studio which he was to call *Le Pig*. The environment in which he now worked undoubtedly had an effect on the content of his new material.

The madman Manson

CHAPTER THREE: PIGGY IN THE MIDDLE

Charles Manson was a failed rock star who had once auditioned to join the Beatles. He had spent most of his youth in state penitentiaries, developing a warped philosophy which he found he could easily apply in the era of love and flower power. He gathered about himself a "family" of devout followers whom he manipulated with sexual politics, hallucinogenic drugs, and the kind of brain washing still used by many mainstream religious cults. His anti-social, anti-American campaign culminated in the murders of Sharon Tate, who was the actress wife of film director Roman Polanski, and four of her friends. The day after the Tate murders, members of the Manson Family killed Leno LaBianca and his wife, who were wealthy owners of a supermarket chain. All the victims had been chosen at random from what Manson perceived as the privileged middle class of white America.

> **Trent would in no way idolize Charles Manson…, though he did find it spookily cool to be connected with an interesting chapter of American history.**

Reznor once again enlisted the production talents of Flood for the new album, and called in a few select guest musicians, including Adrian

Belew, the guitar legend responsible for much of the distinctive sound of the classic David Bowie albums, *Low, Lodger* and *Heroes*. Stephen Perkins, the drummer for Jane's Addiction, then Porno For Pyros, also guested, and Alan Moulder was brought in to lend an experienced hand at the mixing desk.

The single 'March Of The Pigs' was released to critical acclaim, and previewed the forthcoming album, *The Downward Spiral*. By this time, *Pretty Hate Machine* had sold more than a million copies in the USA and nearly 50,000 in the U.K., establishing a big enough army of devout fans to take *The Downward Spiral* straight into the American *Billboard* Album charts at Number 2.

> "I wanted *Downward Spiral* to be a departure from *Broken*... one ultra-fast chunk of death."
> **TRENT**

It seems that people had been fed on substitutes for too long and have been starved of the "real thing." They are so used to the pseudo-art, pseudo-poetry, and pseudo-emotion served up in the sterile environment of popular culture, that they devoured the honesty with which Nine Inch

CHAPTER THREE: PIGGY IN THE MIDDLE

The sane Reznor

Nails address raw emotion, scrutinizing even the uglier aspects of human feelings and desires. In the lyrics of Trent Reznor, love is tied up with hate; motivations are often lacking in honor; guilt and shame influence response. The songs have many more dimensions and far greater depth than the usual boy meets girl pop fare, or the easy Peace & Love political protests. It seems that, although everything is taken from Trent's own personal experience and feelings, he has managed to express basic truths and observations that ring true to many.

Once again, Reznor had flouted pop convention by releasing an album with no immediately obvious singles to be taken from it. The theme of the record follows the descent of an individual through their own inner revelations as they strip away every aspect of their self. Scrutinizing aspects of religion, personal relationships, sex, lies and vices. The album also examines the various ways that the individual tries to hide from itself, divert attention away

> "This time I wanted to make an album that went in ten different directions, but was all united somehow."
> **TRENT ON *DOWNWARD SPIRAL***

from self by various methods, from substance abuse, through the abuse of others, to the abuse of one's self.

It was a kind of personal purging process for Reznor who admits that he "out-bleaked" himself and hopes that he will never get any bleaker. The sound was not just a more extreme development of what had been offered on *Broken* and *Fixed*: it was not an attempt to be louder, faster and harder. Instead the album is preoccupied with texture and mood, stretching the boundaries of what can be done with state-of-the-art sound technology. Using and abusing what is available to produce the results that he wants, not utilizing what the hardware can do, just for the sake of it. *The Downward Spiral* is a technical achievement that has placed NIN at the forefront of the current techno revival.

Trent has stated, "I wanted *Downward Spiral* to be a departure from *Broken*, where I wanted to make a real hard-sounding record that was just one big blast of anger. Not necessarily a well-rounded record... just one

> "On this record I was more concerned with mood, texture, restraint and subtlety." TRENT ON HIS MOTIVATION FOR *SPIRAL*.

In the spotlight—as bleak as ever

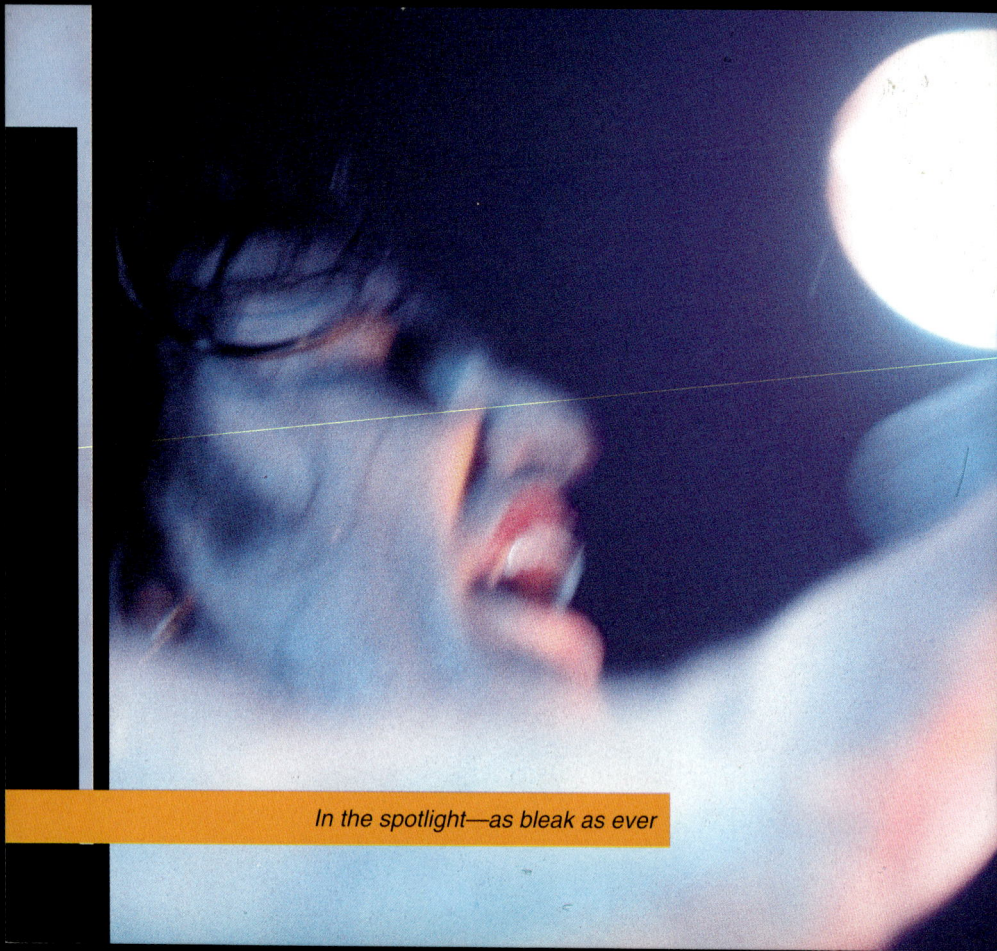

CHAPTER THREE: PIGGY IN THE MIDDLE

ultra-fast chunk of death. This time I wanted to make an album that went in ten different directions, but was all united somehow. I didn't want to box NIN into a corner, where everything had to be faster and harder than the last record, where every song had to say, 'Look how tough we are.' I don't think that's really me.

> By mistake the full uncut version of 'Closer' was played on the U.K.'s most popular radio station, BBC Radio One.

"On this record, I was more concerned with mood, texture, restraint and subtlety, rather than getting punched in the face 400 times. With *Broken*, we wanted to make an album that was just as thick and rich and layered as possible, so that if you listened to it three thousand times, you'd hear a new musical element, a new guitar line every time. With *The Downward Spiral*, we wanted to make a record that was full of holes."

closer to god

The second single from the album was 'Closer', which proved to be the most controversial NIN release to date. The group had become enough of a consistent success that some journalists felt compelled to instigate a backlash. In the U.K., the single caused quite a stir when top radio DJ Bruno Brookes played the wrong version on BBC Radio One, the country's most popular radio station. A special version had been released for radio play with the line "I want to fuck you like an animal" edited out. By mistake, the full version went out across the land, shocking thousands of listeners into complaining and jamming the telephone switchboard.

> "*The Downward Spiral* is the kind of thing I like to listen to when I think the plane is going to crash." TORI AMOS

The accompanying video was the latest and most extreme in a string of controversial promo films, containing scenes of raw meat, pigs' heads on sticks, crucified monkeys and a demonic Reznor screaming obscenities.

An extended release entitled *Closer To God* was put out, containing several remixes and some additional tracks, including a cover version of 'Memorabilia', written by Marc Almond and originally performed by Soft Cell.

Trent took time out to befriend Tori Amos and to provide some backing vocals for the track, 'Past The Mission', from her *Under The Pink* album. To many, this may seem an unlikely combination. Tori admires the work of Reznor and has commented that *The Downward Spiral* is the kind of thing, "I like to listen to when I think the plane is going to crash!"

> "Drugs can be misused, but can also be tools. I think the media needs to be blamed for the glamorization of heroin."
> **TRENT**

rock'n'roll suicide

A month after the release of *The Downward Spiral*, on the evening of April 5, 1994, Kurt Cobain put a loaded shotgun to his head and pulled the trigger. That was how his life ended—not with a whimper, but with a very loud bang.

Born February 20, 1967, Kurt was raised in Aberdeen, Washington, along with younger sister Kim with whom he shared a fairly normal childhood until 1975 when their parents separated. Kurt Cobain and Courtney Love, of grunge rock outfit, Hole, were wed in Hawaii in

Ian Curtis—as bleak as it gets

CHAPTER THREE: PIGGY IN THE MIDDLE

February 1992. Their daughter, Frances Bean, was born in August that year, right into the media circus that focused on Kurt's drug rehabilitation. Reports on Kurt's drug abuse sparked a fierce custody battle, during which Kurt and Courtney fought to prove that they were capable parents. Eventually they managed to win their case.

It was not too long before Kurt reverted to heavy drug use, almost overdosing on at least one occasion. Kurt later locked himself in a room in their Seattle home, threatening to shoot himself. The police were called and after Kurt gave himself up, they recovered several weapons from the premises.

> "Anyone can be a junkie, and there's nothing cool about that. If you don't believe me, hang out with some junkies."
> **TRENT**

The warning signs were clearly there for all to see, Kurt even wrote the song, 'I Hate Myself And I Want To Die'! Like Ian Curtis of Joy Division before him, the management and record companies were blinkered by the dollar signs. They welcomed the constant publicity. Close friends were caught

The legendary Kurt Cobain— another rock'n'roll suicide

CHAPTER THREE: PIGGY IN THE MIDDLE

up in the same meteoric success. Fans identified with his lyrics of tortured alienation... They all missed the point, but sadly, Kurt Cobain did not.

Amid their phenomenal success, Nine Inch Nails found themselves in the shadow of the Seattle scene once more. This time the shadow was a dark shroud. Many parallels have been

> **Kurt Cobain has already been elevated to legend status. To be held in the same esteem as him you have to kill yourself.**

drawn between Cobain and Reznor. In many respects their early years were similar. They both were the product of broken homes. They both have younger sisters. They were both raised in small town USA. Both expressed dissatisfaction with society. Both were quite open about their drug use. Cobain was a serious drug addict. Reznor recognized the potential within himself to develop a serious problem, and has dealt with it while still using cocaine, psylocybin and alcohol on occasions. Both were brilliant and innovative song writers and musicians.

Trent—too strong to be set up

CHAPTER THREE: PIGGY IN THE MIDDLE

Trent has some hard but honest opinions on the subject: "Drugs can be misused, but can also be tools. I think the media needs to be blamed for the glamorization of heroin. Anyone can be a junkie, and there's nothing cool about that. If you don't believe me, hang out with some junkies."

> **Courtney Love proclaimed that Trent wasn't the grunge star he appeared to be, and in fact drove a $100,000 Porsche.**

The music press have tried their damnedest to set Trent up for a rock'n'roll suicide. But he has proved far too strong and stable for that. Trent has been accused of having a morbid fascination with death, suicide and the more desperate elements of the human subconscious. He recorded a cover version of the Joy Division song, 'Dead Souls', for the soundtrack of the movie, *The Crow*. Joy Division's lead singer and songwriter was the awesomely original and talented Ian Curtis, who hanged himself in the early-Eighties. *The Crow* starred Bruce Lee's son, Brandon, who was killed during the filming.

Somehow, even the saddest, most unfortunate tragedy can be glamorized by the rock industry. Kurt Cobain has already been elevated

Not afraid to be vulnerable

CHAPTER THREE: PIGGY IN THE MIDDLE

to legend status and is used as a kind of yardstick against which the sincerity of a musician's angst can be measured. To be held in the same esteem as Cobain as a tortured poet, you have to kill yourself. What people seem to overlook is that Cobain was a very troubled individual, and nothing positive resulted from his suicide. If he was still alive, his songs would be no less potent and effective, only there might be more of them.

> "A lot of music today is just product, written from a video perspective... I find that less interesting than good music."
> **TRENT**

Nine Inch Nails went on tour with *The Downward Spiral* material during 1994, their first live venture for nearly three years. This time the live lineup behind Reznor was Robin Fink on guitar, Danny Lohner on keyboards and guitars, James Woolley on keyboards and Chris Vrenna on percussion. In the Fall of that year, they were joined for six performances by Hole as support. During the latter three gigs, an uneasy interaction

Courtney Love of Hole

CHAPTER THREE: PIGGY IN THE MIDDLE

began between Courtney Love and Trent Reznor. The full truth of whatever went on behind the scenes will never be known for certain. All there is to go on are the many comments from Love and from Reznor and their implications, which do not amount to much at all.

Rumors were spreading that Courtney Love was carrying Trent Reznor's child. This turned out to be untrue. Trent maintains that their relationship never got further than passing each other backstage and exchanging small talk. Courtney proclaimed that Trent was not the grunge star he appeared to be, and in fact drove an automobile worth $100,000. This turned out to be true. He owns a silver Porsche, which he likes to drive dangerously and dice with death. It seems that Courtney was going through a bad phase, for obvious reasons. Now there seems to be no animosity between them: it is just that Trent is the kind of guy that things happen to.

> In 1994, rumors were spreading that Kurt Cobain's wife, Courtney Love, was carrying Trent's child. This turned out to be untrue.

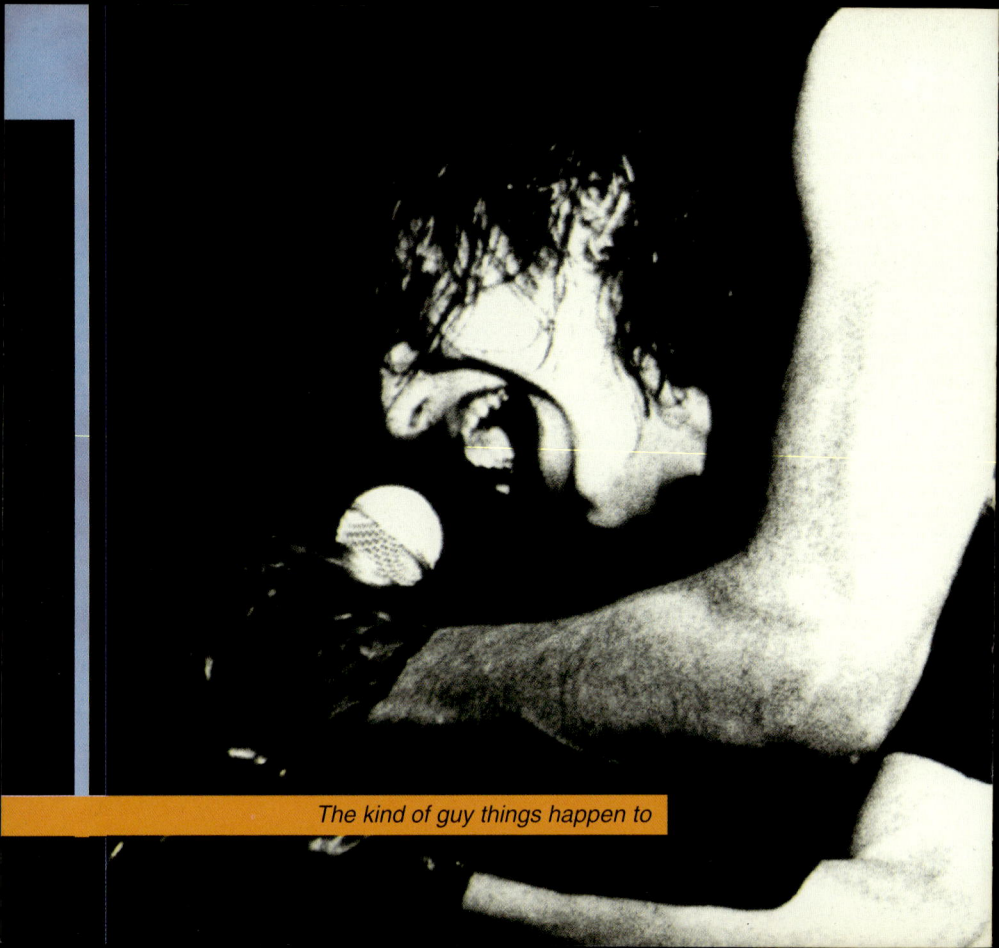

The kind of guy things happen to

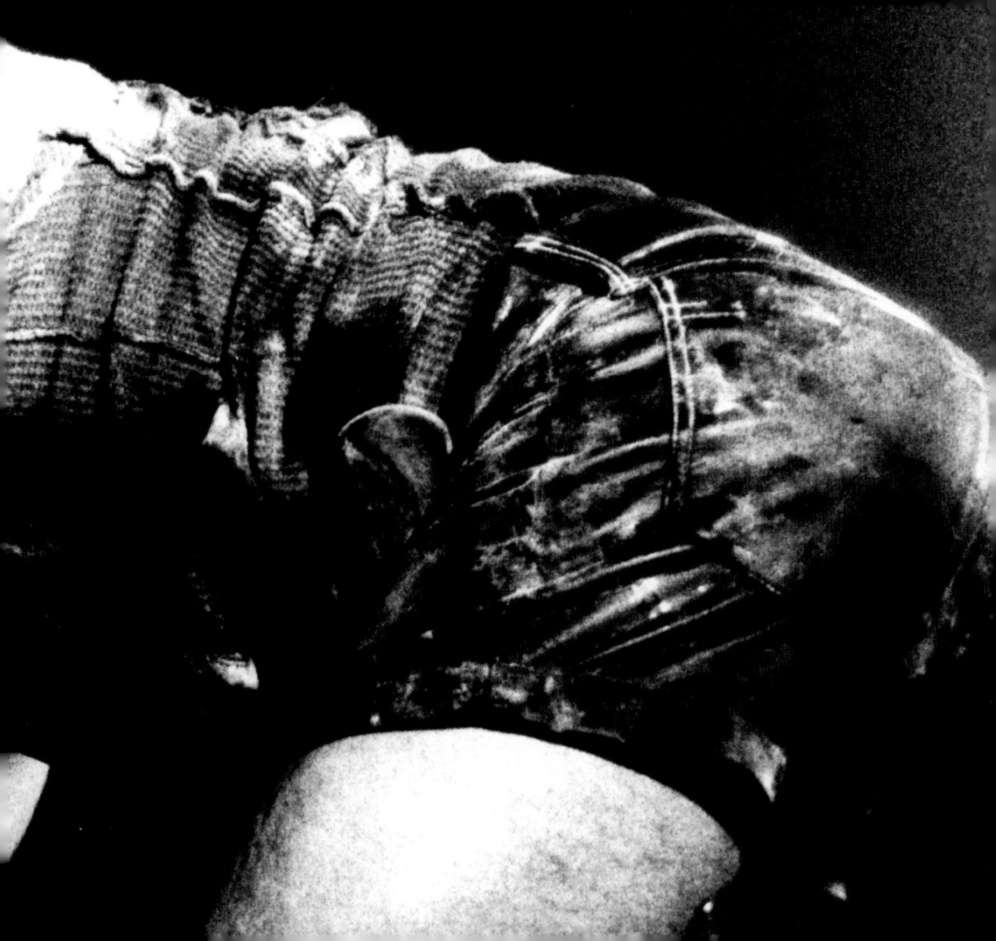

woodstock

The international success of *The Downward Spiral* secured Nine Inch Nails a top billing at Woodstock 94, up with other breakthrough acts like Henry Rollins, The Red Hot Chilli Peppers, Green Day and Porno For Pyros. This was the finishing touch to Trent Reznor's steadily growing celebrity status.

Nine Inch Nails' Woodstock performance was a barely contained explosion of raw emotion and dangerous excitement. The band had been frolicking in the mud backstage, and by the time they took to the stage they looked primal—the mud dried on, cracked off and ran with salty sweat. In the fever of performance, Trent destroyed instruments with menacing glee. The sound that blasted out

> "When I write, I incorporate elements from the fringes of accessibility into something that has mass acceptance."
> **TRENT**

Gritty performance

Fun and games at Woodstock '94

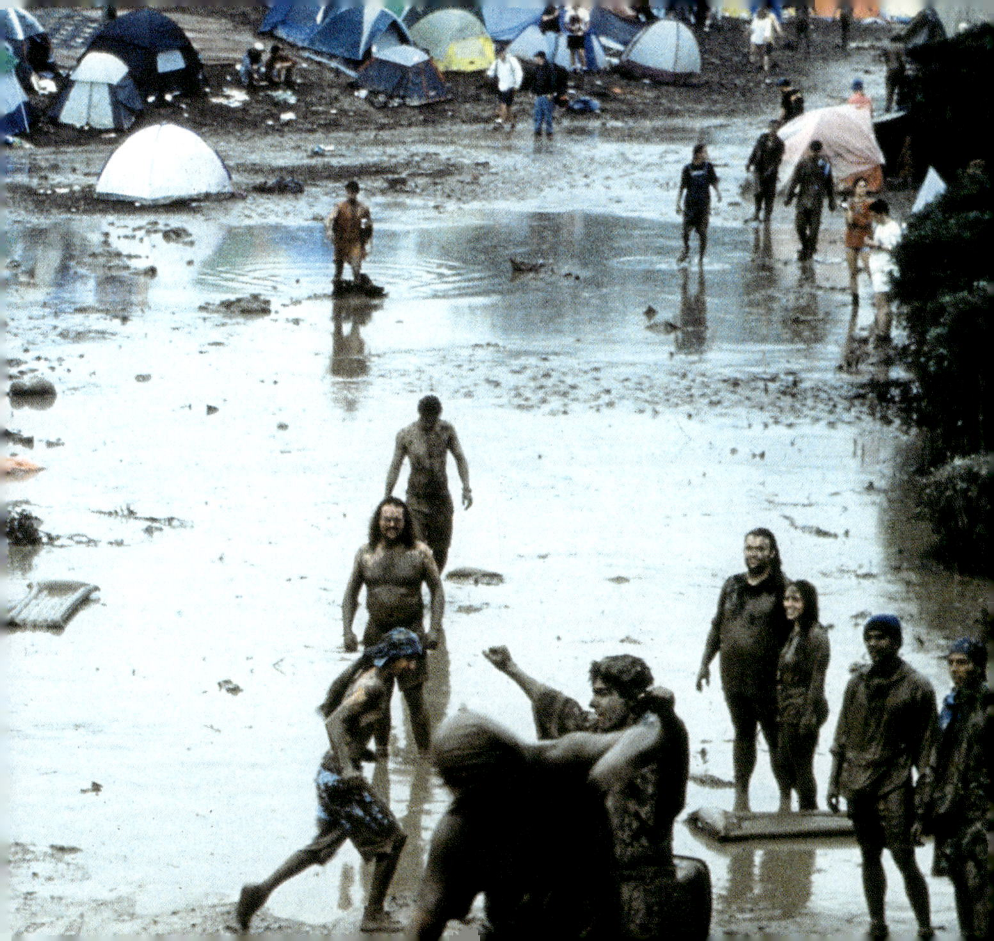

Here's mud in your eye!

CHAPTER FOUR: WOODSTOCK

across the acres of mud-splashed audience reverberated in the chest cavities and groins of everyone.

During the performance, the grit and mud got into Reznor's eyes, making them water. Directly after the show, his eyes watered with the tears of total release and relief. That particular day meant something to Trent that he finds hard to pin down. It could not have been nostalgia: he was not old enough to remember the first Woodstock. Maybe it was what it represented: the Sixties, the time of his early childhood, the long journey from then and there, to the here and now—his own personal history.

Reznor is an artist with good business sense, yet he is unable to explain just what it was that managed to bring NIN across from the regions of experimental rock into the area of mainstream pop. He explains, "When I write, I incorporate elements from the fringes of accessibility into something that has mass acceptance. It's not calculated at all, it's

> "It's [my writing] not calculated at all, it's just that I grew up listening to pop songs, and it's with that structure I work."
> **TRENT**

just that I grew up listening to pop songs, and it's with that structure I work. I found I was using choruses.

"A lot of music today is just product, written from a video perspective. While that can be interesting, I find it less interesting than good music."

The following year, 1995, was Trent's 30th. It started with the release of the fifth single to be spawned from *The Downward Spiral*, 'Piggy'. Also there was a marked departure from the self-examining existentialism we had come to know and need from NIN—a various-artists compilation soundtrack album.

Piggy

Splattered!

"I used to think, naively, that people put out records because they liked music… but it's not about art… it's about ripping people off." TRENT

Any sign of a smirk?

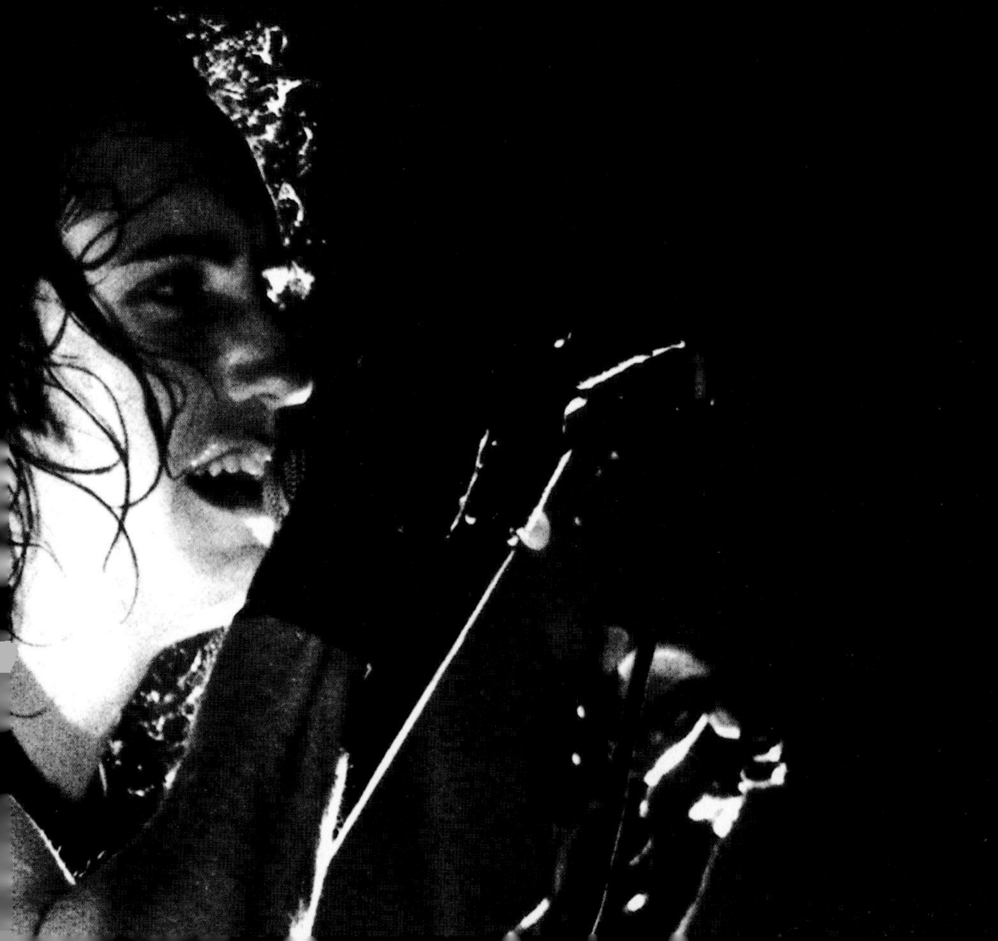

Ministry—early influence with live connections

Trent—flashback

natural born killers

Toward the end of the track 'Sanctified', from the *Pretty Hate Machine* album, there is an almost subliminal monolog. A near whisper recites the words of a letter: "Dear Mom and Dad, this is the hardest letter I've ever had to write. I'd hoped somehow to get out of this quickly so that you'd never have to know about it, but that just isn't possible now. I don't know what's going to happen, but what can I say to you? Will 'I'm sorry' make a difference? Will it ease the pain? The shame you must be feeling? Forgive me. Please." It is a sample from the

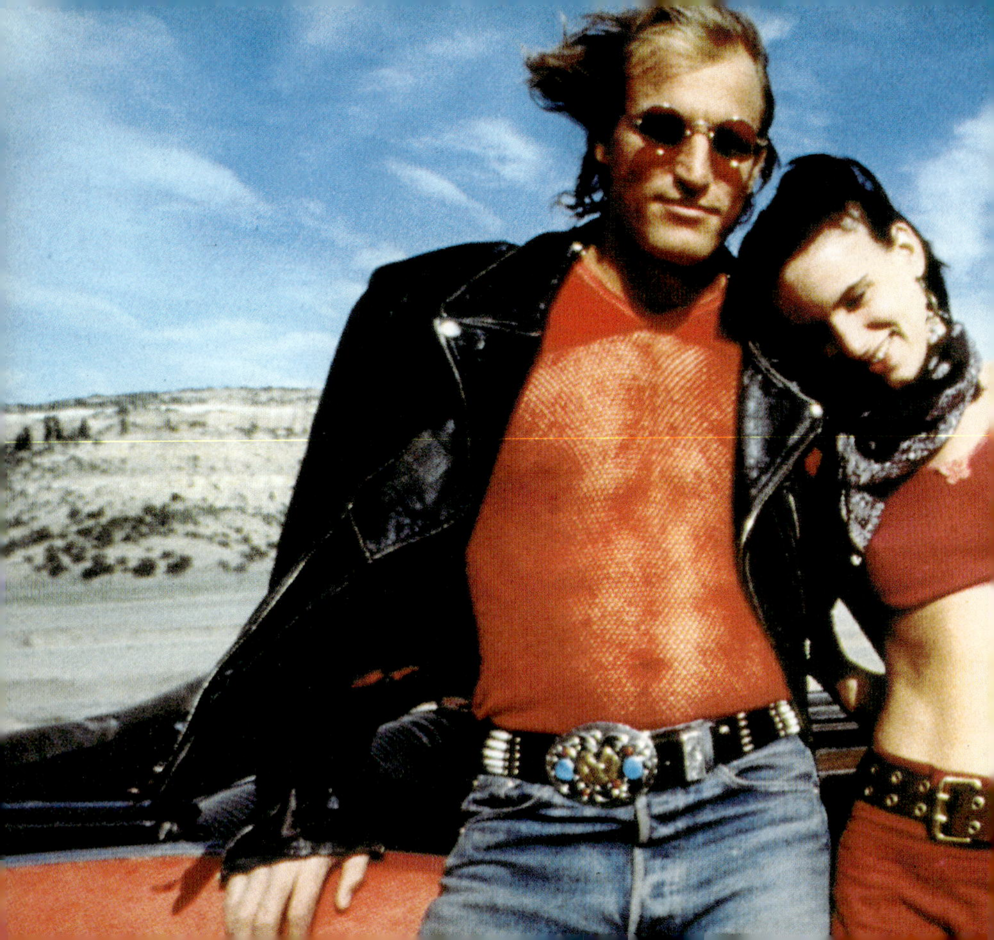

> "I'm interested in composing, whereas basically this [*Natural Born Killers*] was just editing."
> **TRENT**

Natural Born Killers—Woody Harrelson and Juliette Lewis

dialog soundtrack of Alan Parker's movie, *Midnight Express*, which was written by Oliver Stone.

It seems appropriate, then, that Oliver Stone should approach Reznor to compile and produce the soundtrack for the movie *Natural Born Killers*, which Stone adapted from an original script by Quentin (*Reservoir Dogs*) Tarantino. Trent took on the project before he realized that the theme of the film was a serial-killing couple. He had thought the idea sounded cool and had always been interested in movies and in putting music to images.

He used the work as an opportunity for a break after the grueling 12 months of touring that culminated in the Woodstock appearance. The album's production team flew out to Europe and took their studio, which consists of computers and digital recording equipment. Successfully isolated in hotel rooms, surrounded by technology, Trent began compiling the songs that would illustrate the movie. It was a claustrophobic environment that demanded full concentration and an intense approach.

The idea of using so many different artists, reworking some of their songs and remixing most of them, was certainly a difficult task. For the lawyers, it was a contractual obstacle course. As Trent remarks, "Mostly everybody was cool, a couple of snags here and there, but that's to be expected."

CHAPTER FOUR: WOODSTOCK

One major snag was Reznor's contractual obligation to provide new material for the soundtrack. He had never written a soundtrack for anything other than his own internal images. Reznor overcame this obstacle as he does most others: the unstoppable force hitting the immovable object. The resulting offering, 'Burn', was not lacking in NIN integrity.

> "What I'd like to do is work in a totally different format. So for an album there are no videos."
> **TRENT**

The other artists he brought onto the soundtrack were a very unlikely combination, which miraculously went hand in hand to create a cohesive sonic backdrop for the movie. There were the doom-laden poetic monologs of Leonard Cohen, the raw rock'n'roll of the inimitable Patti Smith, the heavy pounding riffs of L7, the vocal acrobatics of Diamanda Galas, the flippant rap of Dr Dre with Snoop Doggy Dog, Jane's Addiction, Patsy Kline, Bob Dylan, even Peter Gabriel, among many others. A lineup which demonstrates Reznor's eclectic and wide-ranging tastes and influences.

Natural Born Killers was instantly notorious. Just having the writer's name, Quentin Tarantino, on a movie could cause an outcry. In the U.K.,

Harvey Keitel in The Young Americans

all films connected to Tarantino had been refused video certification. *Natural Born Killers* was even refused a cinema release in Britain, banned outright pending an inquiry into what may have been a real life

> "I want to put out music that has some integrity to it. Because I tried to do that, I think that's why we got to where we are now."
> **TRENT**

copy-cat killing in France. After several months of delay, no real evidence could be put forward to support its continued hold back, and so the British Board Of Film Classification granted it an 18 Certificate and allowed its release in uncut form.

Trent Reznor has long been interested in creating movie soundtracks, his music has been used in many movies from mainstream teen adventures like *Prayer Of The Roller Boys*, to the Harvey Keitel vehicle, *The Young Americans*. Compiling the rich sound and song collage for *Natural Born Killers* had whet his appetite for more. He has a desire to compose and perform a complete soundtrack, even if it is for one of his own short films. "I'd like to do a real soundtrack," he has admitted. "I'm interested in composing, whereas basically this was just editing. I made a little souvenir of the movie but I don't really feel I've created anything. That, I would like to do... if we ever manage to stop touring."

the future

Trent has always enjoyed experimenting with the video format, though he is often disappointed with the results. In an interview back in 1991 he commented that "...what could have been a cool art form turned out to be nothing but corporate commercials for a record, and it's at the point now where a lot of bands, us included, have to justify quite a sizeable amount of money needed to make a video. What I'd like to do is work in a totally different format. So for an album there are no

Will NIN ever stop touring?

videos—I'll make a film that's 45 minutes long and sell that to stores—and that's the visual accompaniment and that's the way you get to see Nine Inch Nails, and it's a little more special..."

> "I think NIne Inch Nails have a very finite time line, but I'm not worried."
> **TRENT ON PLANS FOR THE FUTURE**

Like any band that criticizes the capitalist commercialism of the record industry, how can Reznor justify his position as a product that has to sell to remain in existence? Surely, he must have made many compromises?

"I used to think, naively, that people put out records because they liked music... but it's not about art, it's not about music, it's about product, ripping people off and marketing schemes and formulas. They want millions of record sales, and I want to put out music that has some integrity to it. Because I tried to do that, I think that's why we got to where we are now, but they don't change the lyrics cos they're a little ugly, let's take those guitars outta the chorus... What's left? I'm just concerned with doing the music as well as it can be done."

NIN have a finite time line

Looking to the future—is that a smile?

As the world heads toward the future, time will reveal what will happen next in the story of Nine Inch Nails. There is a rumor that a live record, or movie is in production. Another album and many more live tours? Trent once commented, "I think Nine Inch Nails have a very finite time line, but I'm not worried."

Nothing remains unchanged. The Tate house has now been demolished to make way for a modern mansion on the same site. Trent Reznor kept the front door as a piece of memorabilia, remembering who had opened that door before him, what had happened behind it and what doors he has yet to unlock.

chronology

1965, May 17	Michael Trent Reznor born in Mercer, Pennsylvania, USA
1970	Tera Reznor born in Mercer, Pennsylvania, USA
	Trent moves to live with grandparents after mother and father divorce
1984	Trent moves to Cleveland, Ohio
1987	Nine Inch Nails release demo version of 'Down In It' independently
1988	Nine Inch Nails sign to TVT Records
1989	'Down In It' released on TVT and album *Pretty Hate Machine*
1990	'Head Like A Hole' single released
	'Sin' single
1991	NIN tour extensively throughout America and Europe
1992	*Broken* is released on Jimmy Iovine's Interscope label after a long contractual wrangle
1994	*Fixed* released
	Trent Reznor moves into the Tate Mansion
	'March Of The Pigs' released
	The Downward Spiral album debuts at Number 2 in the National *Billboard* Chart
	'Closer' released
	Closer To God released
	NIN are a headline act at Woodstock 94
1995	Trent Reznor compiles and engineers the soundtrack for Oliver Stone's movie *Natural Born Killers*
	'Piggy' released

discography

DOWN IN IT (Independent release)
USA: 122 vinyl demo 1987
DOWN IN IT (TVT 2611-2) 17:49
USA: (12"/CD5) TVT Records 1989
(12"/3"CD) TVT Records 1989
U.K.: (CD5 LTD) Island 1990 (CID 482)
(12" LTD) Island 1990 (12 ISP 482)
(AKA: HALO ONE)
1. Down In It (skin) *   3:45
2. Down In It (shred)   6:55
3. Down In It (singe)   7:03
*mix featured on the album *Pretty Hate Machine*.

PRETTY HATE MACHINE 48:50
USA:(LP) TVT Records 1989 (TVT 2610)
(CD) TVT Records 1989 (TVT 2610-2)
(CS) TVT Records 1989 (TVT 2610-4)
U.K.:(CS/LP) Island 1991 (ILPS 9973)
(CD) Island 1989 (CID 9973)
Japan:(CD) East/West 1992 (AMCY-345)
(AKA: *HALO TWO*)
1. Head Like A Hole   4:59
2. Terrible Lie   4:36
3. Down In It   3:45
4. Sanctified   5:48
5. Something I Can Never Have   5:52
6. Kinda I Want To   4:32
7. Sin   4:03
8. That's What I Get   4:27
9. The Only Time   4:47
10. Ringfinger   5:41

HEAD LIKE A HOLE
USA: (12") TVT Records 1990 (TVT 2614)
U.K.: (7") Island 1991 (IS 484)
(12") Island 1991 (12 ISP 484)
(CD5) Island 1991 (CID 484)
(CD5) TVT/Interscope (756785841-2)
Australia: (CD5) TVT/Interscope 1990
Australia
756785812-2 (CSS) TVT/Interscope 1990
Australia 756785814-2
(AKA: HALO THREE)
1. Head Like A Hole (slate)   4:13
2. Head Like A Hole (clay)   4:30

3. Terrible Lie (sympathetic mix) 4:26
4. Head Like A Hole (copper) 6:26
5. You Know Who You Are 5:40
6. Head Like A Hole (soil) 6:38
7. Terrible Lie (empathetic mix) 6:11
(CD5) TVT Records 1990 (TVT 2615-2)
as above plus:
8. Down In It (shred) 6:51
9. Down In It (single) 7:21
10. Down In It (demo) 3:55

SIN 19:32
USA: (CD5) TVT Records 1990 (TVT 2617-2)
(CSS) TVT Records 1990 (TVT 2617-4)
(12") TVT Records 1990 (TVT 2617-1)
U.K.: (7") Island 1991 (IS 508)
(9") Island 1991 (9IS 508)
(CSS) Island 1991 (CIS 508)
(CD5) Island 1991 (CID 508)
(AKA: HALO FOUR)
1. Sin (Long) 5:50
2. Sin (Dub) 4:56
3. Get Down Make Love * 4:17
4. Sin (Short) * 4:19
* Only tracks on the U.S. cassette single

BROKEN 21:01/10:39
USA:(CD5) TVT/Interscope Records 1992
(7-92213-2)
(CS) TVT/Interscope Records 1992
(7-92213-4)
(12") TVT/Interscope Records 1992 (DMD 1903)
U.K.: (7") Island 1992 (IS 522)
(12") Island 1992 (ILPM 8004)
(CD5) Island 1992 (IMCD 8004)
Japan: (CD5) East/West 1993 (AMCY-475)
(AKA: *HALO FIVE*)
1. Pinion 1:02
2. Wish 3:47
3. Last 4:45
4. Help Me I Am In Hell 1:56
5. Happiness In Slavery 5:21
6. Gave Up 4:08
7. Physical (You're So)* 5:30
8. Suck* 5:07
* The Cassette version has the bonus tracks 7 & 8 on side B. The regular vinyl is a single sided six-track 12", with a 7" containing the two bonus tracks.

FIXED 40:22
USA: (12"/CD5) TVT/Interscope Records 1992
(7-96093-2)
(MCS) TVT/Interscope Records 1992
(7-96093-4)

DISCIGRAPHY

U.K.: (CD5) Island 1992 (IMCD 8005)
(12") Island 1992 (ILPM 8005)
Japan: (CD5) East/West 1993 (AMCY-525)
(AKA: *HALO SIX*)

1. Gave Up (remixed)	5:24
2. Wish (remixed)	9:09
3. Happiness In Slavery (remix)	6:08
4. Throw This Away	4:13
5. Fist Fuck	7:19
6. Screaming Slave	8:01

MARCH OF THE PIGS 27:21
(CDS) Nothing/TVT/Interscope Records
1994 (7-95938-2)
U.K.: (CD5) Island 1994 (CID 592)
(CD5) Island 1994 (CIDX 592)
(7") Island 1994 (IS 592)
(9") Island 1994 (9IS 592)
(AKA: HALO SEVEN)

1. March Of The Pigs	2:54
2. Reptilian	8:39
3. All The Pigs, All Lined Up	7:25
4. A Violet Fluid	1:03
5. Underneath The Skin	7:14

THE DOWNWARD SPIRAL 65:10
(CD) Nothing/TVT/Interscope Records
1994 (7-95938-2)
(LTD LP) Nothing/TVT/Interscope Records
1994
(PR 5509)
U.K.: (CD) Island 1994
(2LP)Island 1994 (ilpsd 8012 522 126-1)
Japan: (CD) East/West 1994 (AMCY - 674)
(AKA: *HALO EIGHT*)

1. Mr Self Destruct	4:29
2. Piggy	4:24
3. Heresy	3:54
4. March Of The Pigs	2:54
5. Closer	6:12
6. Ruiner	4:56
7. The Becoming	5:31
8. I Do Not Want This	5:41
9. Big Man With A Gun	1:35
10. A Warm Place	3:22
11. Eraser	4:53
12. Reptile	6:51
13. The Downward Spiral	3:56
14. Hurt	6:12

CLOSER 10:34
(CD) Nothing/TVT/Interscope Records
1994 (PRCD 5636-2)
(AKA: HALO 09)

1. Closer (Radio Edit)	6:12
2. Closer (Clean Pussy Radio Edit)	4:22

CLOSER TO GOD   52:44
(CD) Nothing/TVT/Interscope Records 1994 (7-95905-2)
U.K.:(2 CD) Island/TVT/Interscope Records 1994 (CID 596), (CIDX 596), (12ISX 596)
(2x12") Island 1994 (12IS 596)
(AKA: *HALO NINE*)

1. Closer To God   5:05
2. Closer (Precursor)   7:15
3. Closer (Deviation)   6:15
4. Heresy (Blind)   5:30
5. Memorabilia   7:20
6. Closer (Internal)   4:14
7. March Of The Fuckheads   4:42
8. Closer (Further Away)   5:45
9. Closer   6:25

CLOSER
USA:(CS) Nothing/TVT/Intersocpe Records 1994 (98263-4)
1a: Closer   6:25
2b: March Of The Pigs (live)   3:12

NATURAL BORN KILLERS
USA:(CD) Nothing/Interscope Records 1995 (92460-2)
Soundtrack compiled for the movie, including these tracks written, or heavily contributed to, by Trent Reznor:
8. Burn—NIN
10. Totally Hot—taken from Kipenda Roho by Remmy Ongala & Orchestre Super Matimila
13. Sex Is Violent—Jane's Addiction/Diamanda Galas
15. Something I Can Never Have—NIN
18. Hungry Ants—taken from Checkpoint Charlie and Violation Of Expectation by Barry Adamson
23. Batonga In Batongaville—Budapest Philharmonic Orchestra
24. A Warm Place—NIN
25. Allah, Mohammed, Char, Yaar—Nusrat Fateh Ali Khan

PIGGY   13:03
USA:(CD) Nothing/TVT/Interscope 1995 (PRCD 5923)
(AKA: HALO TEN)
1. Piggy (radio edit)   4:24
2. Hurt (radio edit)   4:37
3. Piggy (rick rubin remix)   4:02

index

A
Almond, Marc 61
Amos, Tori 79

B
BBC Radio One 78
Biafra, Jello 40
Bukowski, Charles 67

C
Cave, Nick 61
Clash, The 20
Cobain, Kurt 79–87
Cocteau Twins 34
Cohen, Leonard 107
Curtis, Ian 81

D
Depeche Mode 33

Dylan, Bob 107

E
Erasure 33

F
Fink, Robin 87
Fox, Michael J. 20

J
Jane's Addiction 107
Jett, Joan 20

K
Keitel, Harvey 109
Kiss 17

L
Leary, Dr Timothy 51

Lee, Brandon 85
Lohner, Danny 87
Love, Courtney 89

M
Malm, John 27, 37
Manson, Charles 67, 71
Ministry 25
Murphy, Peter 31

N
NIN 'Closer'
  controversy 78, 94
  live lineup 87; break
  up with TVT 55;
  choosing the name
  21; comparisons
  with grunge 53–54;
  cyberpunks 49; first

headlining tour 47; first tour 29; Lollapalooza tour 40; Woodstock 94 92
Nirvana 53
Nitzer Ebb 33

P
Parker, Alan 106
Patrick, Richard 40
Pearl Jam 53
Pop Will Eat Itself 59
Prince 25

R
Reznor, Trent birth 12; FBI inquiry 36–40; first record contract 31; first song recorded 27; future plans 110–113; soundtrack for Natural Born Killers 104–109; on Lollapalooza 43; relationship with Courtney Love 89; the Manson house 67
RoboCop 51
Rollins, Henry 45
Rose, Axl, 45
Ruin, Clint 61

S
Severed Heads 25
Simmons, Gene 17
Skinny Puppy 29
Smith, Patti 107
Snoop Doggy Dog 107
Sonic Youth 51
Stone, Oliver 106

T
Tarantino, Quentin 107
Tate, Sharon 67
TVT Records 31

V
Vrenna, Chris 27, 87

W
Ward, Jeff 40
Wonder Stuff, The 31
Wooley, James 40, 87

X
XTC 25